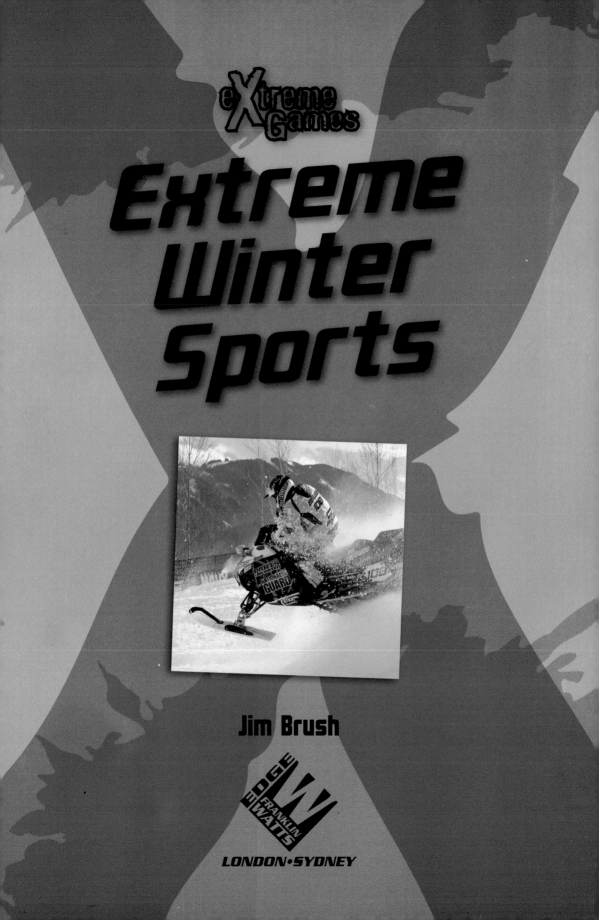

eXtreme Games

Extreme Winter Sports

Jim Brush

EDGE
FRANKLIN WATTS

LONDON • SYDNEY

Series editor: Adrian Cole
Art director: Jonathan Hair
Design: Graham Rich Design
Picture research: Diana Morris

A CIP catalogue record for this book
is available from the British Library.

ISBN: 978 1 4451 0710 3

Printed in China

Franklin Watts is a division of Hachette
Children's Books, an Hachette UK company.
www.hachette.co.uk

The X-Games logo is the property of ESPN, Inc.
CORPORATION DELAWARE ESPN Plaza Bristol
CONNECTICUT 06010. This product
is not endorsed by ESPN, Inc.

Acknowledgements:

Richard Bord/Getty Images: 23, 32, 40.
Bo Bridges/Corbis: front cover. Jean-Pierre
Clatot/AFP/Getty Images: 4, 15, 42, 43.
Jessica Goodman/Getty Images: 8. Jonathan
Moore/Getty Images: 41. Doug Pensinger/
Getty Images: 6, 10, 11, 12, 13, 14, 16,
17, 19, 21, 26, 30, 33, 35, 38. Christian
Pondella/Getty Images: 2, 7, 9, 20, 24, 27,
31, 36, 37. Quinn Rooney/Getty Images: 39.
Kristy Sparow/Getty Images: 22, 34. Jamie
Squire/Getty Images: 28-29. Olav Stubberud,
www.olavstubberud.com: 18.

Every attempt has been made to clear copyright.
Should there be any inadvertent omission please
apply to the publisher for rectification.

Contents

Words highlighted in the text can be found in the glossary.

Welcome to the X-Games

In the Winter X-Games, the world's top winter sports athletes compete to perform the best tricks and earn the fastest times in the hunt for X-Games gold. The winter sports competition showcases snowboarding, snowmobile racing and skiing.

The Winter X-Games are held every year and attract over 200 athletes from around the world. Gold, silver and bronze medals, as well as prize money, are up for grabs.

Snowboarder Shaun White flies through the air during X-Games 14 in 2010. He went on to claim gold in the SuperPipe event.

Levi LaVallee shows why snowmobile racing has become a crowd favourite with a sensational stunt.

The "X" in Winter X-Games stands for extreme. The games are the place for die-hard winter sports stars to show off their most spectacular stunts. In 2006, snowboarder Jeaux Hall tried and failed 17 times before landing the world's first **1080** (three spins in the air). His fellow competitors urged him on from the sidelines. It's all part of the spirit of the games.

eXtreme fact

Being an action sports star takes guts. Take snowboarder Scotty Lago: in the 2011 Winter X-Games he competed in the SuperPipe competition with a broken jaw – and won silver!

Where's the Action?

Over the years, several of the USA's top ski resorts have been used to host the Winter X-Games. In 2010, a new X-Games winter competition was held in Europe for the first time.

The mountains of Big Bear Lake, California.

eXtreme fact

In 1997, Sweden's Jennie Waara became the only athlete in Winter X-Games history to win three medals in the same year: Snowboarder X gold, Halfpipe silver and Slopestyle bronze.

The first ever Winter X-Games took place in January 1997, at the Snow Summit Mountain Resort in Big Bear Lake, California. Athletes competed in ice climbing, snow BMX racing and Moto X; as well as snowboarding. One of the big stars was Norwegian snowboarder Daniel Franck, nicknamed the "Slippery Hotdog", who took gold in men's Slopestyle and silver in the **Halfpipe** event.

Snocross action from Buttermilk Mountain during X-Games 14 held in 2010.

From 1998–9, the X-Games were held in Crested Butte Mountain Resort, USA. Here fans watched new sports, such as stunt, or "Free", skiing, SkiBoarding and snowmobile racing. Since 2002, the Winter X-Games have taken place at Buttermilk Mountain in Aspen, Colorado. Today, more than 80,000 fans attend five days of awesome events.

eXtreme fact

In 2004, the Winter X-Games were televised live for the first time. In 2009, clips of Winter X-Games stars such as Shaun White were made into a stunning 3-D movie.

On the Edge

Rising action sports stars often get their first big break at the X-Games. Here they are encouraged to take risks and to be the first to do a new trick.

Competitors push themselves hard, but if they take a tumble, the other competitors encourage them to have another go. There's always the danger of getting injured. But star status awaits if they can pull off a monster stunt!

Torin Yater-Wallace competing in the Men's Skiing SuperPipe at X-Games 15.

eXtreme fact

In 2011, 15-year-old Torin Yater-Wallace became the youngest winner of a Winter X-Games skiing medal when he earned silver in the Ski SuperPipe event. He beat competitors ten years older than him!

Ashleigh McIvor (in green) of Canada flies over a jump in the Women's Skier X event.

The 2011 Winter X-Games were marked by several big crashes. Attempting a **grab**, Jacob Webster ripped off his ski in mid-air during the Big **Air** event, and slammed onto the ramp. Skier Simon Dumont had a bone-crunching smash onto the **lip** of the SuperPipe, while Olympic gold medallist Ashleigh McIvor had to be carried off on a stretcher after injuring her knee in the Women's Skier X event.

eXtreme fact

Levi LaVallee tried the first double **backflip** on a snowmobile in the 2009 Freestyle Snocross event. He landed it, and became an instant X-Games legend.

Snowboarding Action

Snowboarding has become a hugely popular sport at the Winter X-Games. This is largely thanks to a group of snowboarders in Lake Tahoe, California, USA. They created the first halfpipe in the 1980s.

Nic Suave rides a rail during a practice run for the Snowboard Street event in 2011.

eXtreme fact

In Snowboard Street, athletes compete in a 30-minute **jam** session, hitting urban obstacles such as giant rails. Nic Suave won the first ever event in 2011.

Today, professional or "pro" snowboarders have developed hundreds of new skills and stunts. At the Winter X-Games, snowboarders get to show off their best tricks in events such as SuperPipe, Slopestyle, Big Air and Snowboard Street.

In snowboarding, known as "**shredding**", injuries are common. The competitors wear a range of gear to protect themselves, especially in the Big Air event. This includes: helmets, padding on hips, knees, spine and shoulders; and goggles.

Elena Hight grabs some air during the Women's Snowboard SuperPipe event. Her freestyle board has curved, turned-up ends.

Modern snowboards are made from a wooden core, surrounded by **fibreglass** with steel edges. Many pros use the same freestyle board for the SuperPipe and Slopestyle events. These are short and flexible. The boards used in Snowboarder X are built for speed. They are long, narrow and stiff.

SuperPipe Dreams

The Halfpipe is a classic snowboarding event. In 2001, the X-Games went one better – creating the awesome SuperPipe event.

Shaun White performs a **backside** air in practice. He went on to take gold in the Men's SuperPipe final at Winter X-Games 15.

eXtreme fact

The X-Games SuperPipe at Aspen is 173 metres long. Pro snowboarders can pull off five or six tricks on a course this long.

A halfpipe is basically a U-shaped tube on a downward slope. The SuperPipe is a steeper, bigger version of this, some seven metres deep. This allows snowboarders to get maximum height – or "big air" – above the frozen ground. Competitors link a run of amazing aerial tricks together. The judges look for big air, good style, perfect landings, and how everything flows together.

Landing a move that no one else can do is a great way of getting the judges' attention in the SuperPipe event. In the 2011 Winter X-Games, snowboarder Kelly Clark became the first woman to land a 1080 in a contest.

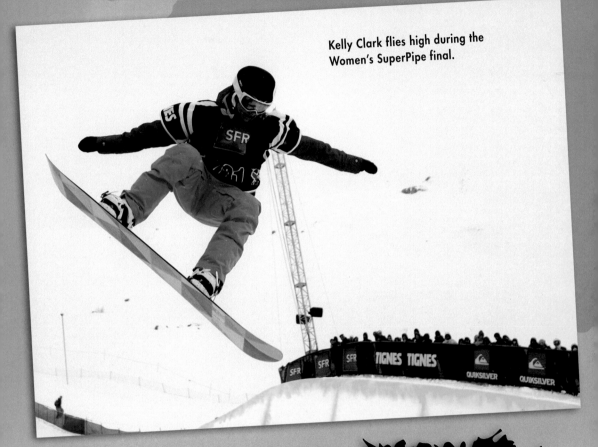

Kelly Clark flies high during the Women's SuperPipe final.

In 2010, Shaun White unveiled his impossibly hard Double McTwist 12 – two flips and three-and-a-half spins. Though the trick helped him to win gold, he famously smashed his face on the lip of the SuperPipe while trying out the move in training.

eXtreme fact

In 2011, Shaun White set a new SuperPipe record by winning four gold medals in four consecutive years.

So Smooth Slopestyle

The Slopestyle course tests a boarder's ability to handle all sorts of different features. It's all about doing a variety of stylish tricks while getting good height off the jumps.

The Slopestyle event is performed on specially made trails at ski mountains. These "**jib** parks" are filled with various jumps, boxes and other obstacles.

The Slopestyle park includes:

- Jib rails, in all shapes and sizes
- Boxes – these are sometimes buses or barrels buried in the snow!
- Joy sticks: poles with a big ball stuck on top

This view of Buttermilk Mountain includes the Slopestyle course (left), SuperPipe (centre) and the Big Air course (right).

The best Slopestyle boarders flow from trick to trick to make their run look smooth and effortless. These include spins, grabs, grinds and flips.

In 2011, at the Winter X-Games Europe Slopestyle event, Chas Guldemond achieved a 99.33 out of a possible 100! This was the highest score achieved by any one in the competition.

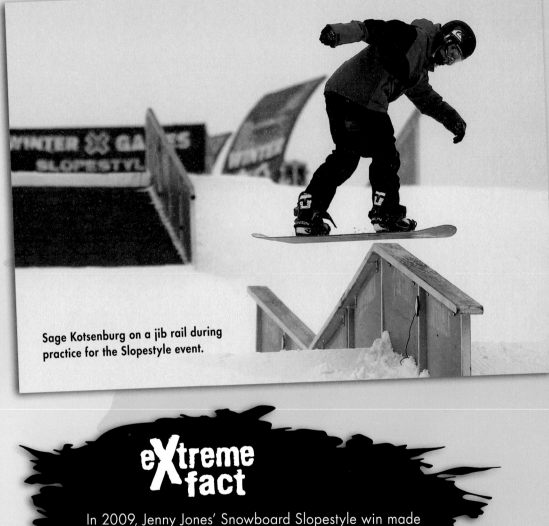

Sage Kotsenburg on a jib rail during practice for the Slopestyle event.

eXtreme fact

In 2009, Jenny Jones' Snowboard Slopestyle win made her the first female Winter X-Games medallist from Great Britain. She won the following year as well in the USA and Europe!

Big Air and Snowboarder X

The crowd-pleasing Big Air event is a chance for the biggest names in freestyle snowboarding to show off their craziest stunts while flying across a huge 26-metre gap!

This sequence photograph shows Torstein Horgmo jumping in the Big Air practice.

The 2011 event summed up what Big Air is all about. Norwegian snowboarder Torstein Horgmo stepped up for this third try at "The Triple", the world's first triple corkscrew. He was suffering from two broken ribs, having fallen hard on his two previous attempts. But with the crowd screaming him on, he soared off the ramp – flipped three times in the air, and landed the trick.

eXtreme fact

In a Snowboarder X semi-final in 2010, world champion snowboarder Max Schairer of Austria had to be taken to hospital after a nasty pile-up with two other boarders.

Snowboardercross, or Snowboarder X, is a mix between snowboarding and Moto X. Six boarders race head-to-head down a 1,100-metre long course, snaking around tight turns and over jumps. All the time they are looking for places to pass. First down to the bottom wins!

Accidents – or **wipeouts** – in Snowboarder X are common. More injuries occur in Snowboarder X than almost any other event at the Winter X-Games.

Seth Wescott (centre) leads the way in the X-Games 15 Men's Snowboarder X.

Snowboard Stars

In its short history, the Winter X-Games has been dominated by snowboarding sensations such as Shaun White and Lindsey Jacobellis.

Shaun White

American Shaun White is one of a kind. He has won a medal at the Winter X-Games every year since 2002, including 17 golds and 11 other medals by 2011. In 2009, he captured his fourth straight Slopestyle title, then in 2011 pulled off the same feat in the SuperPipe event. His red hair and fancy airborne moves earned him the nickname the "Flying Tomato"!

Shaun White holds up his snowboard to the crowd after winning gold in the Men's Snowboarding SuperPipe in January 2011.

eXtreme fact

In 2007, Shaun White became the first person to win a gold medal at both the Summer and Winter X-Games.

Lindsey Jacobellis displays her gold medal after her win in the Women's Snowboarder X, in 2011.

Lindsey Jacobellis

"Lucky" Lindsey Jacobellis first entered the X-Games at the age of 15 and has won the Snowboarder X gold an incredible seven times, including a run of four victories in a row. Jacobellis is also known for her great attitude. She famously lost out on Snowboarder X Olympic Gold after she crash-landed on the next-to-last jump trying a fancy move. She said afterwards, "I was just having fun, and I messed up."

eXtreme fact

In 2006, unstoppable Slopestyle competitor Janna Meyen-Weatherby became the first Winter X-Games athlete ever to **four-peat** in a single event.

Let's Party!

The atmosphere at the X-Games is very special. As well as death-defying stunts, there are live music events at the X Fest, celebrity spectators and competitions for fans.

Competitors gather at a press conference for the Winter X-Games.

eXtreme fact

Mono skier Josh Dueck summed up the spirit of the X-Games: "It's a community feel. Everybody is working with each other to make sure that everyone has their best performance and they put on a good show."

Tens of thousands of fans turn Aspen into one big party for the X-Games – despite the freezing weather! The X-Games last for five days, and they're free. Screaming fans can watch several events at once on monster-sized TV screens.

In the Snowskate Park, young fans get the chance to show off their skills on rails and ledges, or try out the latest gear. There's also the chance to meet the stars face-to-face and get their autograph. Some fans wear T-shirts over their winter coats, covered in athletes' signatures!

eXtreme fact

In 2002, 380 out of 470 students failed to show up for school when the X-Games was first staged in the resort. Since then, Aspen's school students are given the Friday of the X-Games off.

Skier, Kevin Rolland, signs autographs for waiting extreme sports fans.

Sled Mayhem

Snowmobiles, also known as sleds, **are capable of eye-popping stunts, 30-metre leaps – and truly spectacular crashes. All in all, a perfect match for the Winter X-Games!**

Modern snowmobiles are fast and powerful. They can reach speeds of 120 kph or more in under four seconds. They are popular with fans because the riders perform incredible stunts.

Snowmobile racing made its first appearance at the Winter X-Games in 1998, followed by the Freestyle, and Speed & Style competitions.

Riders wear a wide range of protective gear including:

- Helmet
- Gloves
- Goggles
- Leather boots
- Shin and knee guards
- Elbow pads
- Neck braces

Snowmobile riders face extreme dangers. Imagine one of those heavy, bone-crunching machines landing on top of you! In 2011, medal favourite Heath Frisby crashed out of the Freestyle event when his right arm slipped out of the hold. This made his body twist and he was ripped off the sled.

eXtreme fact

Snowmobile events can be dangerous for officials too! During the Snocross finals in 2011, Bobby LePage's snowmobile flew off the course after a bumpy landing. It crashed into official Val Meyer, knocking him off his feet.

Levi LaVallee during practice for the Freestyle snowmobile competition.

Crazy Flipping Freestyle

Snowmobile Freestyle is one of the most jaw-dropping events of the whole X-Games. Bulky 200-kg machines doing backflips in the snow has to be seen to be believed!

Justin Hoyer kicks out in mid air in the Freestyle event at Winter X-Games 15.

Freestyle snowmobile riders, nicknamed "sled necks", can make the tricks look easy. But they risk their lives every time their machines take off into the air, especially when doing upside-down or "inverted" stunts.

eXtreme fact

To add to the thrills, athletes don't have to say in advance what stunt they are going to perform. Fans never know what is coming next.

In the Freestyle event, the judges look for runs that are smooth and controlled. In 2009, the left ski on Justin Hoyer's machine landed just outside the jump area. It cost him gold – though he came back to win the event in 2010.

The Next Trick competition sees snowmobile riders pulling out their biggest stunts. In 2010, Heath Frisby won gold with his Tsunami flip (above), in which he "ran" beneath his upside-down sled in mid air!

eXtreme fact

For years, Caleb Moore had raced all-terrain vehicles. In December 2009, he swapped from wheels to skis. Incredibly, just a month later he won bronze in the Winter X-Games Snowmobile Freestyle event!

Snocross and Speed & Style

Snocross is all-out snowmobile racing. The racers compete on tracks made up of tight turns, banked corners, steep jumps and obstacles.

The competition is always fierce in Snocross. The first courses were longer, with deeper holes and higher jumps. Modern courses are built for speed. Even so, the jumps are up to nine metres high, making the riders soar up to 40 metres before landing again – with a thump.

The start is all-important, as the winner is often quickest through the first turn, known as the "**holeshot**". Once they get going, the sleds can reach speeds of up to 100 kph.

Snowmobile Speed & Style combines the air of Freestyle and the speed of Snocross in a single event. Pairs of competitors zoom around the course hitting side-by-side ramps. After four laps of racing, the rider who crosses the finish line first wins the speed portion. But the rider finishing second can still win if his style score is high enough to make up the difference.

Riders accelerate away from the starting line in a Snocross competition.

eXtreme fact

In 2011, a new Snocross event was included in the Winter X-Games – Adaptive Snocross. This ran on the Snocross course, with a few changes, to suit snowmobile riders with disabilities. Mike Schultz of the USA won gold.

Snowmobile Monsters

The stars of the snowmobile events have provided many unforgettable moments, like Aleksander Nordgaard's record-breaking 32-metre backflip in the Freestyle event in 2007.

Tucker Hibbert

In 2000, Hibbert defeated reigning champion, Blair Morgan, a five-times X-Games gold medallist whose stand-up, high-flying style changed the sport forever. Hibbert went on to dominate the sport, winning a remarkable five golds in a row from 2007 to 2011.

eXtreme fact

Tucker Hibbert won gold in the 2000 Snocross event aged just 15, becoming the youngest gold medallist in Winter X-Games history.

Tucker Hibbert flying to victory in the Snocross competition at X-Games 15.

Daniel Bodin

In 2011, Daniel Bodin performed the first ever Double Grab flip. He has appeared in the snowmobile Freestyle event every year since it was added to the X-Games in 2007.

Levi LaVallee

Freestyler Levi LaVallee first made the headlines when he won two gold medals at the 2008 Winter X-Games. The next year, he became the first person in history to attempt a double backflip in competition.

eXtreme fact

Some of the top freestyle riders train in indoor foam pits to keep their newest tricks hidden from other competitors. The foam also gives them a softer landing!

Preparing the Course

Preparation for a Winter X-Games event starts a long time before the athletes and fans show up at the venue.

This Snow Cat is fitted with a 6.45-metre high Zaugg Pipe Monster.

A lot of work goes into building the various courses. All of the snow features for the Winter X-Games, like the SuperPipe, jumps and giant **moguls**, are sculpted from machine-made snow. Special vehicles, called Snow Cats, scoop snow into position. Then huge arms, called Pipe Monsters, are used to shape the curved sides of the SuperPipe.

eXtreme fact

Snow machines turn water into tiny droplets using a jet of high-pressure air. When the droplets are blown into freezing air, they become snow crystals.

Every course has to be just right to get the very best out of the competitors. A laser measure is used to check the curve of the SuperPipe slope. The Slopestyle course changes every year. It takes ten days or more to build it. Snow ramps are created, and rails and boxes are put into place.

This is part of the Winter X-Games course at Buttermilk Mountain. The Snowboard Street course is at the front, with the snowmobile course behind it.

Freestyle Skiing

Mind-blowing stunts performed by freestyle skiers at the Winter X-Games have raised the profile of skiing. It's now just as cool as snowboarding.

There were no skiing events at the first Winter X-Games in 1997. But around this time, **twin-tip** skis became available. Their upturned tips and tails allowed skiers to perform stunts backwards, or "**fakie**". Soon skiers were performing jumps, grabs and grinds just like snowboarders.

Canadian Justin Dorey catches some air off the SuperPipe.

eXtreme fact

In 2007, Peter Olenick performed the first ever double-flip in the Skiing SuperPipe event. Nicknamed the "Whisky Flip", it led to a new era of even more amazing tricks.

Freestyle skiing became part of the X-Games in 1998. The first Big Air event was held a year later. This was followed by Slopestyle and SuperPipe in 2002. Since then, freestyle skiing has continued to grow, thanks to **pioneers** like Tanner Hall and John Olsson.

Simon Dumont on his X-Games gold medal-winning run in 2004.

The Skiing SuperPipe competition takes place on the same giant U-shaped pipe as the snowboarding event. Every year the stunts get bigger and better. In 2004, Simon Dumont rose 6.7 metres above the deck to win Skiing SuperPipe gold.

Skiing Big Air and Slopestyle

The Winter X-Games showcases the most exciting freestyle skiers in the world. The Skiing Big Air and Slopestyle events are a feast of crazy flips and spins.

Bobby Brown almost disappears into the night sky during the Ski Big Air event.

The Big Air event has always been one of the biggest crowd-pullers. In the 2010 event, T J Schiller landed the first-ever double corked 1620 – that's four-and-a-half spins in the air. Unbelievably, it wasn't enough to win gold! In only his second Winter X-Games, 18-year-old Bobby Brown stepped up and achieved a perfect score of 100, performing two tricks that had never been landed before in competition.

Kaya Turski launches down the start ramps on the Ski Slopestyle course.

eXtreme fact

Canadian skier Kaya Turski won the first Women's Slopestyle Skiing competition in 2010, with the highest ever Slopestyle score at a Winter X-Games of 96.66.

In the Slopestyle event, skiers combine big air and technical tricks into one run. They follow the same course as snowboarders, combining spins, grabs, grinds and flips.

The judges score highly for style and control. In the 2011 event, many competitors had trouble with the fast Slopestyle course. But after all three runs, Sammy Carlson took gold in the men's competition.

Downhill Dynamos

Skier X and Mono Skier X are more like traditional downhill skiing events. But there's no shortage of drama as four competitors race head-to-head on a fast and furious course.

Kelsey Serwa (above) crashes down with Ophelie David (top right) during the Women's Skier X final.

The Skier X, or Skicross, course combines steep slopes with jumps and gates. Though pushing and pulling are banned, spectacular collisions add to the thrills. In the 2011 Women's event, Kelsey Serwa and Ophelie David were neck-and-neck at the last jump. They got tangled during the landing and wiped out. Luckily for Serwa, she slid across the finish line first and won gold.

Mono Skier X features mono skiers with disabilities racing over tabletop jumps, banked turns, rollers and gaps. Like Skier X, there are lots of crashes and wipeouts. In the 2011 final, two out of four skiers fell. The final jump is huge, with skiers leaping 25 metres or more.

eXtreme fact

In 2011, veteran mono skier Chris Devlin-Young became the oldest athlete to compete at the Winter X-Games, aged 49.

Josh Dueck won gold in the Mono Skier X in 2011.

Skiing Supremos

There's no shortage of skiing superstars at the Winter X-Games.

Tanner Hall

Tanner Hall is probably the biggest name in Freestyle skiing. He earned his first Winter X-Games gold in 2001. By 2008, he had become the only person to "three-peat" in two Winter X-Games events, adding three straight Skiing SuperPipe wins to his Slopestyle victories.

eXtreme fact

In 2005, doctors said Tanner Hall might never ski again after breaking both ankles jumping over the notorious 36-metre wide Chad's Gap in the wilds of Utah, USA. It didn't stop Hall claiming gold at the X-Games Superpipe the next year!

Simon Dumont

With eight X-Games under his belt, Simon Dumont (above) is best known for his great height in the SuperPipe competitions. In 2008, he became the world record holder for the highest ski air on a **quarterpipe**, at 10.6 metres.

Sarah Burke

Canadian skier Sarah Burke won her fourth gold medal in the Women's SuperPipe competition in 2011. She is also the first woman to land a 1080 in competition.

Ophelie David

French skier Ophelie David (above) is the queen of Skier X, winning gold four years in a row from 2007 to 2010 – the first skier to do this. She is also a very talented mountain biker.

X-Games Europe

In 2010, for the first time the Winter X-Games Europe (or WXE) competition came to Tignes in France.

Perhaps the highlight of the 2010 event was the Double McTwist 1260 landed by Swiss snowboarder Iouri Podladtchikov, known as the "I-Pod". He only began practising the trick a week before. This gave him the gold medal in the SuperPipe with a giant score of 98.0. British snowboarder Jenny Jones also continued her winning streak in the Women's Slopestyle event by taking gold.

Norway's Kjersti Oestgaard Buaas flies high, with the winter resort of Tignes, France, in the background.

The European event was repeated the following year. Some 70,000 fans flocked to see three days of competition, with 150 athletes competing in skiing and snowboarding SuperPipe and Slopestyle events.

eXtreme fact

In 2010, a Zaugg Pipe Monster machine had to be shipped across the Atlantic to build the 220-metre long SuperPipe course at Tignes, as it was the only machine in the world big enough.

Kevin Rolland performs an "Iron Cross" at X-Games Europe.

One of the crowd favourites at the 2011 Games was French skier Kevin Rolland, who won the SuperPipe. In the women's event, Kelly Clark claimed her third gold medal with a superb, aggressive run.

X-Games medal tables

Winter X-Games 15 (2011)	1st	2nd	3rd
Snowboarding			
Men's Slopestyle	Sebastien Toutant	Mark McMorris	Tyler Flanagan
Women's Slopestyle	Enni Rukajarvi	Jenny Jones	Jamie Anderson
Big Air	Torstein Horgmo	Sebastien Toutant	Sage Kotsenburg
Men's SuperPipe	Shaun White	Scotty Lago	Louie Vito
Women's SuperPipe	Kelly Clark	Kaitlyn Farrington	Elena Hight
Men's Snowboarder X	Nick Baumgartner	Kevin Hill	Nate Holland
Women's Snowboarder X	Lindsey Jacobellis	Callan Chythlook-Sifsof	Deborah Anthonioz
Street	Nic Sauve	Louis-Felix Paradis	Simon Chamberlain
Best Method	Scotty Lago	Ross Powers	Chas Guldemond
Snowmobile			
Freestyle	Daniel Bodin	Justin Hoyer	Caleb Moore
Speed & Style	Joe Parsons	Heath Frisby	Cory Davis
Snocross	Tucker Hibbert	Ross Martin	Robbie Malinoski
Adaptive Snocross	Mike Schultz	Jeff Tweet	Jim Wazny
Best Trick	Daniel Bodin	Caleb Moore	Heath Frisby
Skiing			
Men's Slopestyle	Sammy Carlson	Russ Henshaw	Andreas Hatvelt
Women's Slopestyle	Kaya Turski	Keri Herman	Grete Eliassen
Men's SuperPipe	Kevin Rolland	Torin Yater-Wallace	Simon Dumont
Women's SuperPipe	Sarah Burke	Brita Sigourney	Roz Groenewoud
Big Air	Alex Schlopy	Bobby Brow	Sammy Carlson
Men's Skier X	John Teller	Chris Del Bosco	Casey Puckett
Women's Skier X	Kelsey Serwa	Ophelie David	Fanny Smith
Mono Skier X	Josh Dueck	Brandon Adam	Sean Rose

Websites & Glossary

http://espn.go.com/action/xgames/winter/2011

The awesome ESPN gateway to their Winter X-Games coverage, including videos, photo galleries, competitor biographies, interviews and results. Plus a mobile app (so you can stay up-to-date with everything happening on the scene), podcasts and Twitter feeds.

http://www.lindseyjacobellis.com/index_flash.html

Lindsey Jacobellis' website featuring photos, videos and links to her blog pages.

http://www.tucker-hibbert.com

The website of Tucker Hibbert, which includes his biography, a photo gallery, his blog, race results, videos and free downloadable wallpapers.

http://tannerhall.com

Tanner Hall's website is packed with photos, movies, competition results, plus his biography and the latest news.

Please note: every effort has been made by the Publishers to ensure that these websites contain no inappropriate or offensive material. However, because of the nature of the Internet, it is impossible to guarantee that the contents of these sites will not be altered. We strongly advise that Internet access is supervised by a responsible adult.

1080, 1260, 1620 – Aerial spins. A complete spin is 360 degrees, so a 1080 is three spins.

Air – Short for aerial. Any time an athlete and their equipment gets airborne.

Backflip – A backward somersault in the air.

Backside – The side of a board where a snowboarder's heels sit.

Fakie – Riding backwards to your normal stance.

Fibreglass – A strong, lightweight material made from various plastics strengthened by glass fibres.

Four-peat – Winning an event four times in a row. A five-peat is five wins in a row and so on.

Grab – When an athlete grabs the edge of their board, skis or snowmobile during an aerial stunt.

Grind – Sliding along the top of an obstacle such as rail or lip of a ramp.

Halfpipe – The U-shaped pipe used in the X-Games Superpipe events.

Holeshot – The first corner on a Snocross racetrack.

Jam – Timed session, such as 10 minutes long, in which athletes take turns to perform stunts.

Jib – Sliding on rails or other platforms with the snowboard.

Lip – The top of a jump.

Moguls – Bumps deliberately built into a course.

Pioneers – The first people to try something out.

Quarterpipe – A single wall of the halfpipe, used in Park courses and in Big Air events.

Shredding – Slang for snowboarding down a hill.

Sled – Another name for a snowmobile.

Twin-tip – Snowboards and skis whose nose and tail are both pointed so that athletes can ride equally well in either direction.

Wipeout – A dramatic fall.

Index